Red Zone
American Football Logos
Coloring
Book

Red Zone
American Football Logos
Coloring
Book

This Book Belongs To:

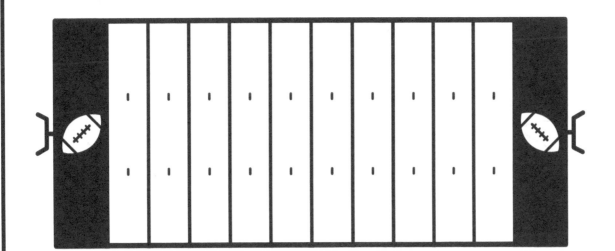

Test Page:

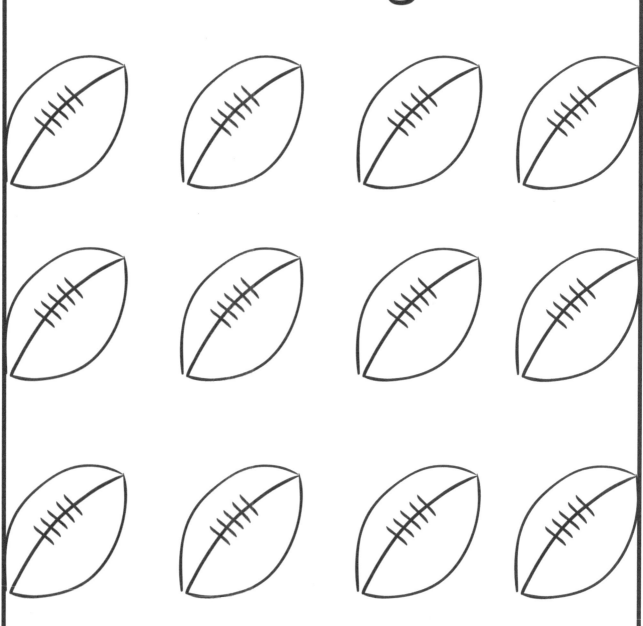

Assessment

Your support and trust mean a lot to us and we hope that **RED ZONE AMERICAN FOOTBALL LOGOS** is completely enjoyable and allows you to enjoy football and your favorite teams as much as we enjoy doing it for you.

WE VALUE YOUR OPINION.

If you like the book, we invite you to leave a review on Amazon. Your opinion is very important to us and allows us to continue improving.

3

Index

NFC
East

Dallas Cowboys

8

New York Giants

10

Philadelphia Eagles

12

Washington
Commanders

NFC
North

Chicago Bears

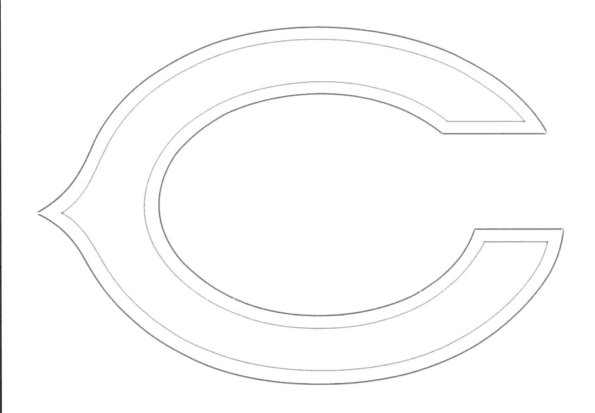

17

Detroit Lions

Green Bay Packers

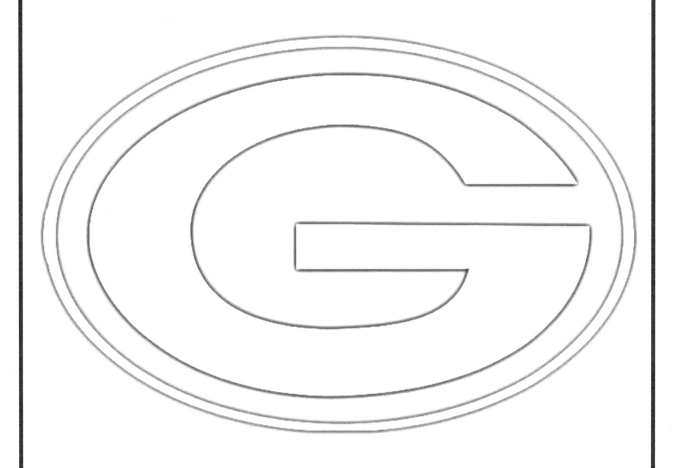

21

Minnesota Vikings

23

NFC
South

Atlanta Falcons

Carolina Panthers

New Orleans Saints

30

Tampa Bay Buccaneers

NFC
West

34

Arizona Cardinals

35

Los Angeles Rams

San Francisco 49ers

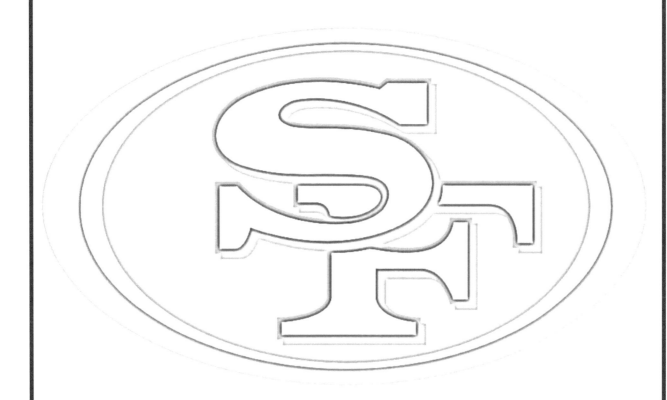

39

Seattle Seahawks

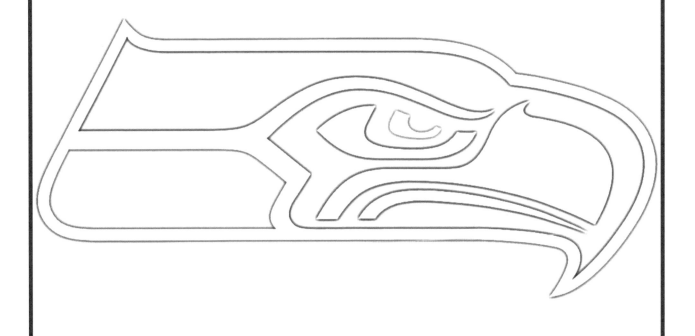

41

AFC
East

Buffalo Bills

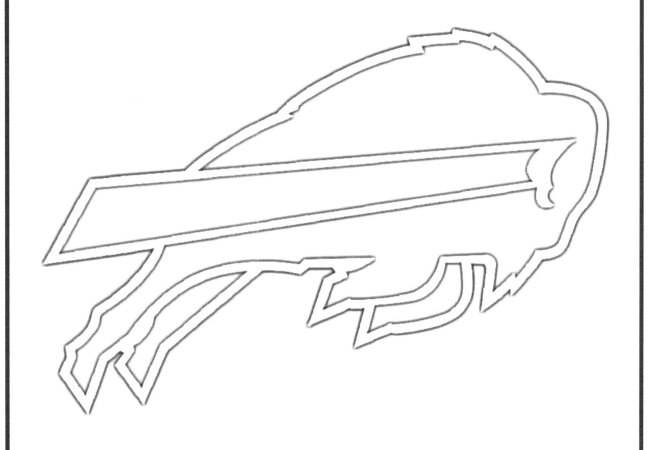

46

Miami Dolphins

48

New England Patriots

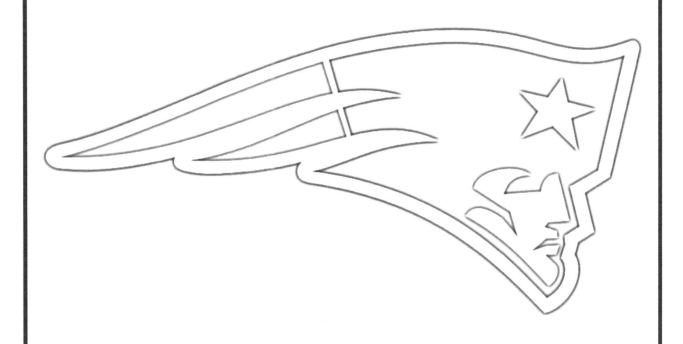

50

New York Jets

52

AFC
North

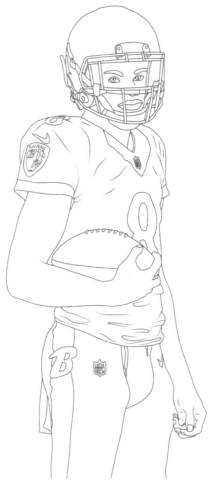

Baltimore Ravens

Cincinnati Bengals

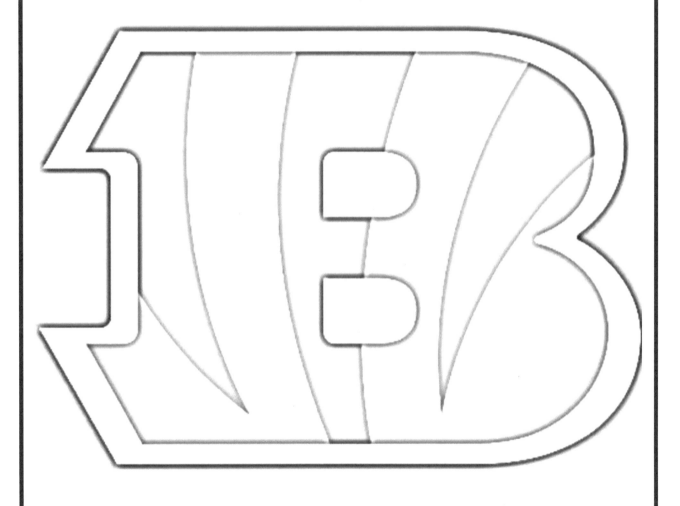

57

Cleveland Browns

Pittsburgh Steelers

AFC
South

Houston Texans

64

Indianapolis Colts

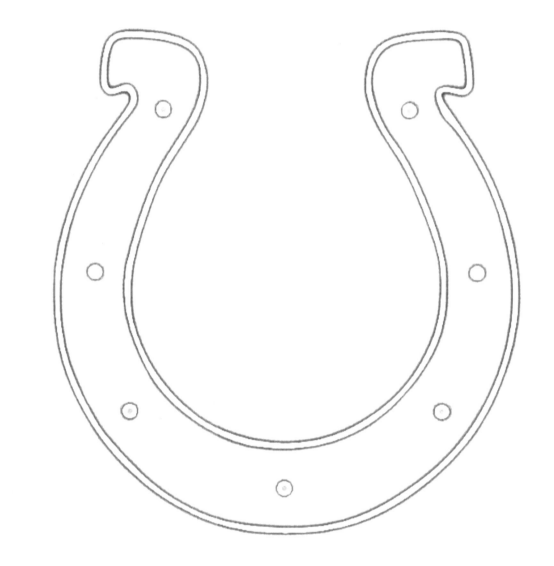

66

Jacksonville Jaguars

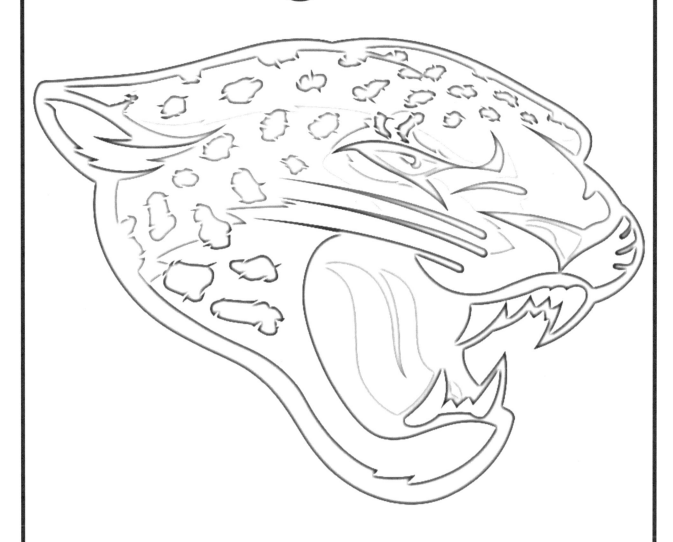

Tennessee Titans

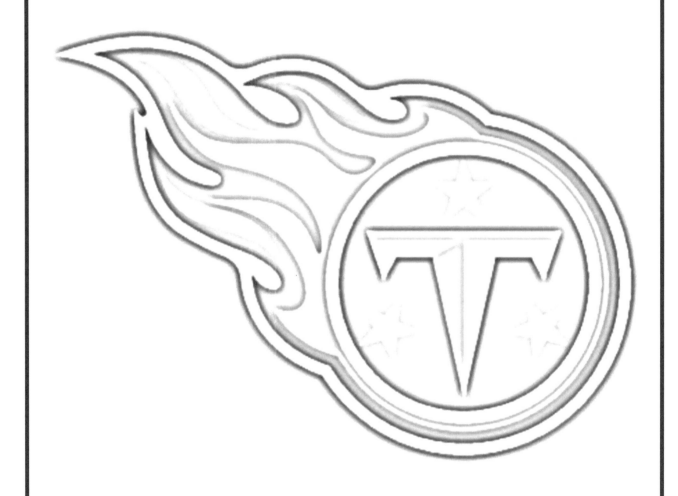

70

AFC
West

Denver Broncos

Kansas City Chiefs

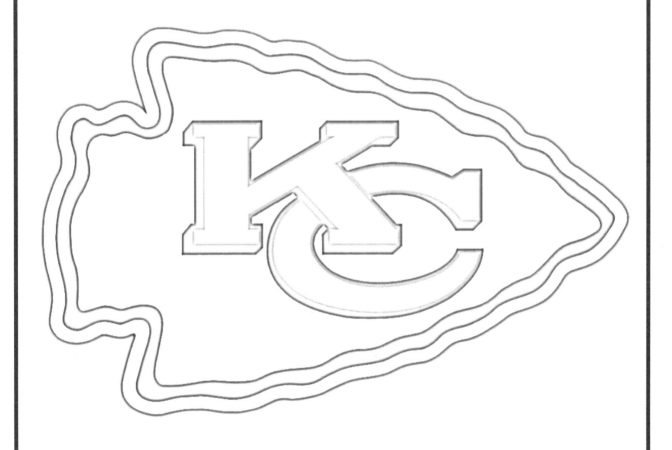

75

Las Vegas Raiders

77

Los Angeles Chargers

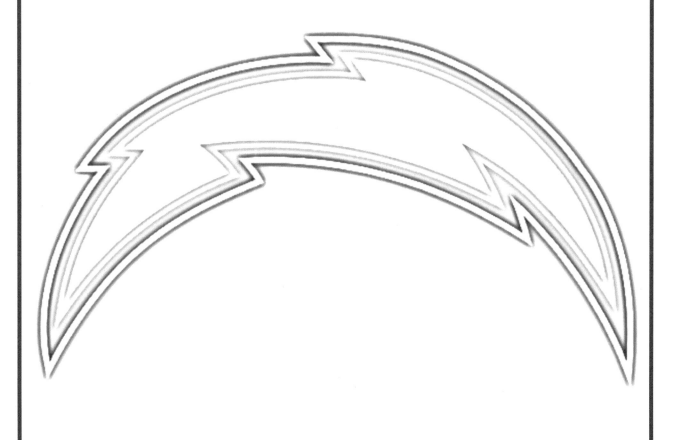

79

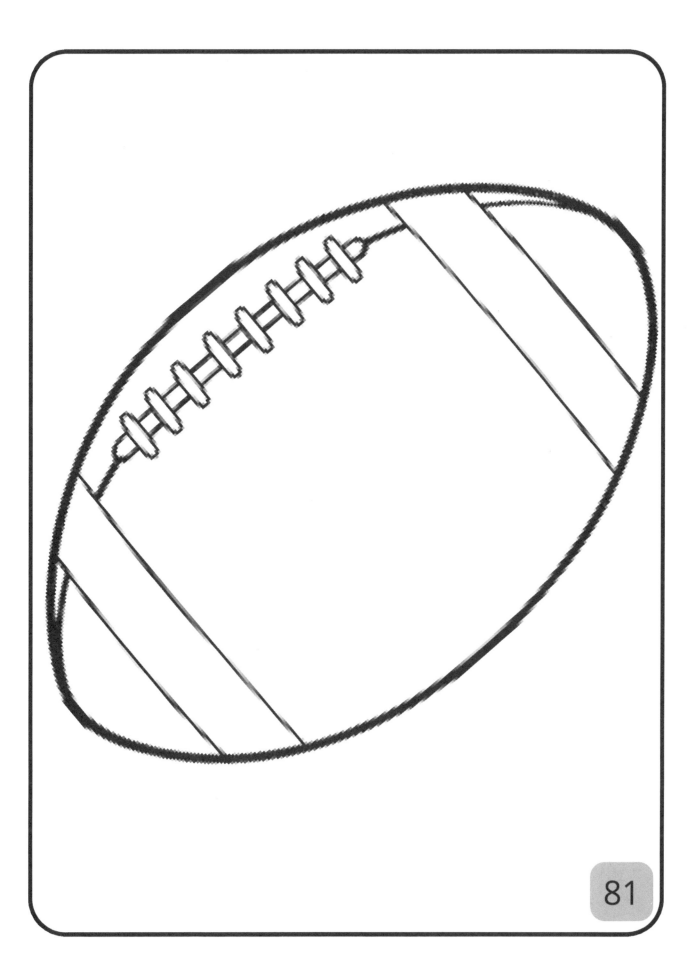

81

NFC EAST

Dallas Cowboys   Washington Commanders

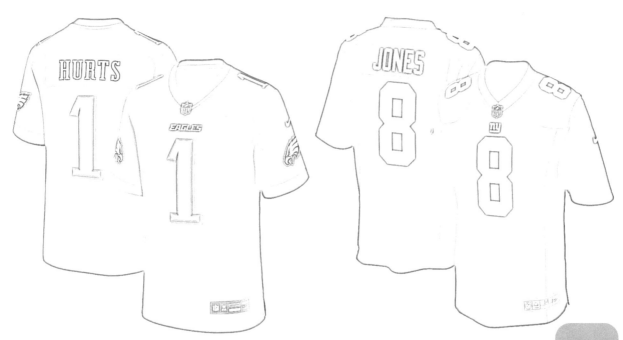

Philadelphia Eagles   New York Giants

NFC NORTH

Chicago Bears

Green Bay Packers

Detroit Lions

Minnesota Vikings

85

NFC SOUTH

Atlanta Falcons

Tampa Bay Buccaneers

New Orleans Saints

Carolina Panthers

NFC WEST

Arizona Cardinals

LA Rams

Seattle Seahawks

San Francisco 49ers

AFC EAST

Buffalo Bills

Miami Dolphins

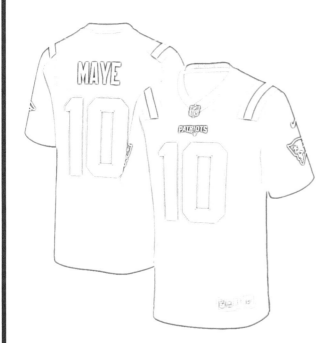

New England Patriots

New York Jets

91

AFC NORTH

Baltimore Ravens

Cincinnati Bengals

Pittsburgh Steelers

Cleveland Browns

93

AFC SOUTH

Houston Texans

Indianapolis Colts

Jacksonville Jaguars

Tennessee Titans

95

AFC WEST

Denver Broncos

Kansas City Chiefs

Las Vegas Raiders

Los Angeles Chargers

Are you a sports fan?
Keep having fun and learning with our other books!

Go to our books section

Made in United States
Troutdale, OR
12/11/2024